BINARY TRADING STRATEGIES

Learn Binary Options Profit Making Strategies

WAYNE WALKER

Table of Contents

INTRODUCTION 7

CHAPTER 1: The Basics of Binary Trading 9

CHAPTER 2: Fundamental Analysis 13

CHAPTER 3: Technical Analysis 19

CHAPTER 4: Basic Options 25

CHAPTER 5: Signals and Technology-Based Strategies 31

CHAPTER 6: Co-integration Strategy 35

CHAPTER 7: Selecting a Trade Partner 39

BONUS: Tech Analysis Trade Guide 43

CONCLUSION 59

PROFILE OF THE AUTHOR... 61

INTRODUCTION

ongratulations on your personal copy of *Binary Trading Strategies: Learn Binary Options Profit Making Strategies.*

This book will ensure that you are equipped to begin binary options trading and execute the strategies that go along with them. It will examine several techniques that can increase your profit making ability. The final chapters will explore strategic moves that you can begin using right away. The bonus contents will take you even further! There are plenty of books on the market, thanks again for choosing this one.

CHAPTER 1:
The Basics of Binary Trading

Binary options are often referred to as trading options that are either all or nothing and with good reason, this is because of the way that they work. **Binaries differ from plain vanilla options because their payoff is a fixed amount and based on a yes/no proposition.** This duality of possible outcomes for binaries is what gives them their name. They are capital markets instruments that many people have chosen to use in their quest for profits.

The main challenge with binary options trading is that many people are not quite as profitable as how they could be. This is due to the fact that they are unfamiliar with the strategies that they can use to maximize profits from their trades. If you intend to trade binary options or only just thinking of starting to trade them, you need to make sure that you are prepared. You prepare by reviewing and learning the different possibilities that you have with the strategies that we will cover.

All

The "all" factor plays into the desire to trade using binary options for many people. You are able to make a good amount of money just from a few trades and that will give you other trading possibilities with your new profits. With binaries you don't have to guess about what you can make or not make depending on the market. At the beginning when you open a binary option trade, you will know exactly what you might be able to gain from the option. You will either make that amount or in many cases you will not make anything. If you were enticed by the fact that you will get a set amount back, you may want to also take a look at the other side of binary trading.

Nothing

If you don't make all of the money back that you put into it (and more), you will make nothing. There is always that chance with binary trading and that can be a huge problem if you don't have the capital to spend on trades. For this reason, you need to ensure that you have adequate risk capital so that it would not have a huge impact on you if you were to lose on one trade. While you can binary trade as a new trader, it may not always be your best option because you stand the chance of losing all of the risk capital that you put in. This is one of the downsides to binary trading and something that you need to be aware of.

There are several strategies though that will help you to become profitable from these types of options. Whether you want to increase the likelihood that you will make money or simply want to learn the specifics that go along with making profits from binary trading, using these strategies can be beneficial for anyone who uses them.

CHAPTER 2:
Fundamental Analysis

Most people who trade or are involved with the markets use fundamental analysis to some extent. When you begin executing the various trading concepts presented later in the book, this analysis will assist you to do even better. Fundamental analysis is a tool that you will use with almost every other strategy. As you give yourself the opportunity to explore new concepts and learn about the different things that are possible with binary options, it is a good idea to use fundamental analysis to help you along the way.

Basics

The basic idea behind fundamental analysis is that you look at a business or a stock as a whole. You need to figure out the information on the balance sheets, along with the cash flow and every other relevant aspect of the business. You will use this information to balance the risks/rewards that come along with investing in it and this will help you to have a better understanding of the business. Is it worth investing in, or should you pursue different opportunities with the money that you have?

Cash Flow

Cash flow is one of the key areas that you will examine when you are using the fundamental analysis model to help secure profits with the binary options strategies. Is there a positive cash flow? Are any unusual issues accounted for and explained? If the answer to either of these is "no," you will need to figure out why and then decide whether or not this will be a good opportunity for you.

Length of Time in Business

The length of time that a company has been in business can have an impact on the amount of money that you can make from it in a specified period of time. If a company has not been in business for a long time, it may not be the best idea to choose to invest in them. The same goes if it has been in business for a very long time – there is an expiration date on everything, and the business might need to close if it has not kept up with the changes in the marketplace.

Debt Level

Debt level is another of the factors to take into consideration when deciding to invest in a company. You want to look for what is called a low current asset to current liabilities ratio. Normally a ratio in the area of 1 to 3 is ok.

In some cases however, too much cash can be negative. It can be a sign of several things; they are not investing enough in the future, nothing is in the product development pipeline. Excess cash could also mean they are not looking to make any strategic buys. Many say it is a sign of not enough proactive thinking on the part of the company's leadership.

Keep in mind that the ratio is relative to the sector that you are researching, for example, companies in the tech sector have debt ratios several times higher.

PE Ratio– Price to Earnings ratio

This is how much a company is worth on an exchange in relation to income from its product and services. This is the most used method of valuing shares (stocks) to see if they are priced right. You will hear the term repeatedly so it is important that you understand this concept. Using a simple example, if a firm has shares that are valued 50 million and the profits are 5 million, the P/E ratio is 10. As we discussed with assets to liability, the ratio is relative to the sector that you are researching.

Directors Trading

Directors are required to disclose when they trade shares in their companies. They are usually the most informed in the company so it might be a clue to future events, but keep an open mind.

Some people will say directors are selling because there is something negative going on in the company, or they are buying because there are aware of something positive. It is an indicator but it is not a 100%, for example, if selling, it could be something as mundane as they need the money. They might want to invest in other things or they are over exposed to that particular company's shares and need to reduce. It also could be due to a divorce therefore it is not always a clear sign that something dramatic is happening.

Tax Information

When looking at the fundamental analysis basis behind the business that you are hoping to invest in, you can also look at taxes. Looking at taxes from the past and the present is helpful if you are going to invest in a business and plays a role in the bigger picture of it. If there is no way for you to see the taxes or if something appears unusual about the taxes of a business, reconsider if this firm is for you.

Projected Profits

There are many methods that you can use to figure out what the likely profit will be for a chosen company. You can use them, and the majority of the time, you will find the information that is needed through your investigations. If you are unable to forecast a profit in the near future you may want to consider a different company to invest in.

The Big Picture

Always look at the big picture of the investments that you are considering. The bigger picture should provide you the information that you need and will help you assess the best use of your funds. Combine all of the information that you have collected and piece them together. Does it seem like the business is stable? Are there expected profits? What does the future hold for the business? Each of these things will help you to figure out what might happen and whether or not you should make the choice to invest. You never know exactly what the market will do so keep that in mind when you are investing.

This strategy is one of the best that you can use. It encompasses all things relevant that you need to know about a business, and it is something that nearly all investors use when considering to place a trade or invest. Finally, you don't have to use just one strategy (fundamental analysis), and in fact, using two strategies can help you to make more profits from trading binary options.

CHAPTER 3:
Technical Analysis

While the names are similar, there are actually quite a few differences between the fundamental analysis and technical analysis strategies. This is because of the different things that they focus on and the way that they are able to leverage the advantages that comes with each of them. One of the biggest benefits of using technical analysis is that you don't have to worry about the actual value of a company (or asset) – only about the profits that the asset might bring you when you invest in or trade it. For this reason, you will have less work to do when you are figuring out your next steps.

The Past

The important thing that you will examine when you use technical analysis are prior price movements of the asset. You will need to see past market movements and the way that people were able to make money from them. This is also a good way to ensure that the stock or currency pair is actually volatile enough to make a profit for you when attempting to forecast how much the price will go up or down.

There is much that you can learn from past price movements of an asset and the way it reacted to market events, for example, a company earnings report. Next, you need to assess if there are adequate money-making opportunities based on the way that the stock performed. If investing for longer term, make sure that you primarily choose investment opportunities that were profitable in the past because they stand a better chance to continue to be so in the future.

Prediction of the Future

Another benefit that comes from looking at past price movements of an asset is that you will actually be able to make a more informed decision about the future of it and the various ways in which it could make you money later on. This is essential if you want to make sure that you are profiting from your trades.

Binary options can be a gamble, therefore, you need to reduce your chances of making poor trades. However, technical analysis is a solid tool that will help you to analyze the information that can influence the way that your trades might perform. Knowing ahead of time that a company is likely to perform well (or poorly) makes your odds of selecting the right calls and puts much better. Even with all the information, you do need to be careful, because market movements can be extremely unpredictable and there can be misjudgments.

No Financial Statements

It can be difficult at times to deal with financial statements, taxes, and other information on the different areas that a business has. For this reason, people may not want to use fundamental analysis, they instead choose technical analysis. It does not work the same way, but it can provide results that are just as positive and it gives investors the ability to make better decisions without having to spend hours reading documents for the information they need. These advantages are another reason why technical analysis is often a more attractive option for some traders and investors.

If you are worried about the accuracy that comes from trading or investing without knowing every single aspect of the business's financial past, you can be assured that you will benefit from technical analysis.

Technical Analysis Tools

Bollinger Bands – Technical Analysis Tool (1)

Bollinger bands are a tool that many investors and traders use when they want to add different technical analysis aspects to the binary options that they have. They are used to measure market volatility. The bands define the upper and lower limits of the trading range. When you view the bands on a chart, you will have a top and a bottom band, the space between the top and the bottom, many people call this the buy – sell channel. You use the space between the bands to get an idea of where you are within the trading range. So if you are near the top, you know that you are close to the resistance level and there is a potential for a price reversal (the market changes direction). If you are at the bottom, you know that you are near the support level for a potential price reversal there.

For the most part prices do remain between the bands. If the price begins to break out, people take this as a signal so you do need to be aware of that.

Moving Average – Technical Analysis Tool (2)

Similar to the Bollinger band, the moving average indicator is normally included with your various charting options. When you look at the moving average graph you will be able to see the average price movements of the asset that you are analyzing. This will provide you information of not only where the tradable prices were, but also where the company price average was in relation to the sales that they had (if trading stocks). The average price is a key piece of information that will help you to determine the likely success of the trade, so make sure that you are taking it into account when mulling over several trade ideas.

Moving averages (MA) are mostly useful because they make it easier to spot a trend. This is key with stocks, foreign exchange, or some of the other derivatives where an up market is great and a down market can also be great. With these asset classes all we need to do is to identify or spot this trend. For example, a fifty-day moving average adds up the closing prices for the last fifty days, divide by fifty and plots a point on the chart for each day. If looking at a moving average chart and you have MA ten, MA fifty, ten is the short term, fifty is the long term.

The shorter moving average, if that is above the longer, the trend is considered upwards. If the shorter moving average is below the longer moving average, then the trends is considered downwards.

Relative Strength Index – Technical Analysis Tool (3)

The RSI, which is the Relative Strength Index is used to identify if the market (stock, currency pair, etc.) is overbought or oversold. It has an index from zero to one hundred. The RSI matches more or less what is happening on the chart and it should. Readings below thirty indicate that the market maybe oversold and when you see or hear the term oversold it mean excessive selling. Readings above seventy indicate that the market maybe overbought, excessive buying. Keep in mind these are indications, they are not guarantees of anything. As a note, the market can remain overbought or oversold for a considerable period of time. The RSI is a leading indicator, it begins giving signals before the trend has begun.

NOTE: These are only the basics within technical analysis, clearly to go further you will need more time with this and that is recommended, especially with short term trading. Please see the bonus technical analysis guide at the end of the book to broaden your knowledge even more.

CHAPTER 4:
Basic Options

A Call Option

When you buy a call option, you have the market view that the price of a stock, a currency, a commodity contract, etc. will rise before the listed expiration time. Traditional options make this more difficult because they require that you estimate the degree to which the price of the asset will rise within a certain amount of time, but binary options simplify this by making it simply a question of whether the price will go up or down by a certain point in time. So, to recap: if you believe that the price of a stock (or related asset) will go up, you will buy a call option.

Put Option

Put options work similar to calls, but in the opposite direction. If you believe that the price of an asset is heading lower, you will buy a put. A put indicates that it's going to drop an amount within x amount of time as indicated by the expiry date. Your goal, in order to make money off a put options contract, is to predict accurately when you believe that an asset's value will fall.

Safeguarding

It is NOT possible to guarantee that you will not lose some of your money when you are trading binary options, but there are some things that you can do to help safeguard the money that you have and increase your odds. For example, the basic options hedging strategy is what you will be able to use while you are getting started with your trading.

Underlying Asset (Basic hedge strategy)

The first thing that you can consider is to trade in the underlying asset so that you have more than one stream of capital that is going into the trade. The trade that you do with the underlying asset will serve as the part that will protect you in the event that you begin to lose some of your money on the option. An example would be that after buying a put option, you then buy the underlying stock. Your purchase of the put indicates that you expect the stock price to fall, if your analysis was incorrect and the stock climbed higher, your purchase of the stock would protect you. In other words you have hedged your position.

By putting your money in two different avenues, you can potentially cash in twice. However, the amount that you can profit depends on the options that you have, the hedge ratio (between the option to the underlying stock), and with the various expenses for the execution of your trades.

Stop Losses

Stop loss orders that you use with stocks, for example, some brokers offer variations of these orders that can be used with binary options (Please be aware, stop losses are NOT a common feature of options trading).

In general, the stop loss order is used to mitigate one's losses by setting a point at which the stock or other asset will be sold if you bought or bought if you sold at the start of the trade. More is lost initially when trading binary options simply by nature of the fact that the *amount* lost doesn't particularly indicate the amount of personal *investment* lost, as binary options are essentially bets on whether the price of a commodity or asset will rise or fall.

Making Money

The way that you make money from your trading is going to depend on the strategies that you are using. It can be challenging at times to make money so keep all of that information in mind while you are trading. If you were not able to make sufficient profits or if you experience excessive losses from the capital that you have, you won't be able to move forward and that can put a halt on your options trading career.

Short-Term Necessities

Since there is a lot that is going on with binary trading and the opportunities that you have, you will soon see the benefits that come along with short-term trades and the way that they work for various strategies. If you want something that is going to be a long-term trade within the binary options market, you can consider using the basic strategy. It can help you create a better chance at having a winning trade and you will probably lose less money.

Starting Small

It is always best to start small. Even if you do have a lot of capital that you can use with binary options, you shouldn't put it all in. Putting a lot of money in upfront is a very risky strategy and something that is not recommended. Instead, if you want to profit long term, you should put a little money in at the beginning, make profits from that amount and then put more money in each time that you collect on the profits that you have earned from each trade.

Top Reasons Why Traders Lose

The top three reasons why traders lose. First is no plan, as they said in the old days "failing to plan is planning to fail", that is true when you are dealing with trading. The examples of this no plan comes from personal experience of dealing with new traders. Some of the stories I have heard are almost unbelievable, I would ask people "why did you place this trade?" with money that they probably worked hard for, I have heard, "my cousin told me to do it", "I heard about it at a barbeque", really almost unbelievable things or basis for placing the trade. Therefore, if you have no plan the results will reflect this.

The second reason is what I call too much risk. The too much risk is the person, who is trading binary options, foreign exchange or some derivative product where you can have situations of up to one hundred, two hundred or three hundred times leveraging. If they actually max this out and use all the available leverage, then definitely it's going to be some risky trading ahead. You do want to take a look at your risk or margin exposure and as mentioned in my classes, that you want to ensure that failure is survivable.

The final reason is confusing trading with investing. Here you will find many times that people will take this competition approach, saying trading is better than investing, I say it depends on what you are doing. If you are trading, and for me if you are trading that means you have a relatively short time frame. For example, with day traders, they will open and close trades within a day therefore they use the tools that are applicable for this, like technical analysis. If you have a longer time frame heading into investing territory, from a year, five years, ten years, then you will use the tools for that. Taking scalping or day trading techniques and putting them into your investments is not a good strategy.

CHAPTER 5:
Signals and Technology–Based Strategies

There are some strategies that require you to do so little work that the computer will actually do most, if not all of the binary options trading for you. This is the idea behind auto-trading which is something that people did not have access to in the past because of the lack of needed technology.

All you need to do with these programs is put in the risk capital that you want to trade, and then you will have the money traded automatically. It gives you the chance to try more strategies with your binary options while you work toward initial profitability.

Algorithms

These are tools that will assist you to execute binary options trades that hopefully will get you into profitable territory. They can be a good thing if you do not like or want to make a lot of decisions about the different binaries that are available to trade. Algorithms can also be used in a plan to generate passive income.

It is a good idea to investigate the different types of trades that will be performed according to the algorithms, the point here is to make sure that you do your research. It can be difficult at times to understand how the programming which is behind the algorithms works, so make sure that you are aware of that fact before you try and use them. It is strongly recommended to do some *basic manual* trades before you get started so that algorithmic trading is not the first thing that you do.

The trading approach that is taken by an algorithm is different than if you were binary trading by phone, which was how much of trading was done in the past. An algorithm is working with numbers and codes while continuously scanning the overall market for trading opportunities. A game of numbers such as options trading comes somewhat naturally to it; as a result, the margin of error on a very well-written binary options trading program is much lower than that of a human.

One of the challenges that exists for algorithmic trading is that people simply don't have as much experience with algorithmic-based binary options trading as they do with traditional trading. You will need to choose carefully from the options algorithms that are available on the market.

Signals

There are different binary signals providers that will tell you when you should trade and how you should adjust the settings of your executed trades. These signals can include suggestions on:

- Stop Loss
- Entry Levels
- Profit Taking
- Buy/Sell Stop Orders
- Limit Orders
- Market Orders

Each of the providers have different approaches to signals and they will have different signals on the areas that they are specialist in. Whichever one that you select, you must be able to trust in the signals that comes from them and the trade suggestions they make available.

Be sure that you are using a signal that is compatible with the trading platform that you have. There are some signals which will not work with certain platforms. Signals can be tricky, so learn as much as you can about them before you use them with your trading. Despite the fact that you are using signals, you should still consider having a broker that has the resources to help you with trading options if needed. Binary trading, no matter how automated it becomes, it can still be tricky sometimes.

Applications

While algorithms are really convenient for people who want to automate the trading that they do with binary options, you can take even greater advantage of capital markets technology when you use the apps that are available. You can try the different applications to help you get the maximum benefits out of your options. They will help you not only to have an easier time with trading but also allow you do it all on the go. Applications are easy to use, combine a lot of different properties, and give you a chance to see your trades in real time no matter where you are located.

If you chose to use applications for your binary trades, make sure that you start out with them gradually and early in your trading career so that you can avoid having to make major switches as you become more experienced. A note to keep in mind, given how relatively new the technology is, be sure that the application you decide to use is well reviewed by fellow traders.

CHAPTER 6:
Co-integration Strategy

There are many asset classes that you can select from when you are starting out with binary options. This strategy will give you the chance to explore as you become more experienced and figure out exactly what methods work for you.

The idea is to find two assets (stocks, currency pairs) that are similar to each other and are correlatively related, whether due to a related industry or something of the like. This will allow you to notice when there is a difference in the two and you can profit from the difference (gap) that is between them.

Finding the Assets

The basis of this entire strategy is finding two stocks or assets that are related, identify a gap between the two and then use it to your advantage. Whenever there is a gap, for example, between two highly related stocks, it will often close. How quickly it closes depends a lot on market volatility.

The majority of the time, you will be able to find forex pairs that are similar and run along similar paths but there is a noticeable gap that exist between them. Forex and stocks are the types of assets that you can use with the co-integration theory. By looking at the different asset classes and gradually figuring out how co-integration works, with some practice, you can make a decent profit. Look at the different binary options by asset class so that you can find the two best applicable stocks or currency pairs to use when assembling your co-integration strategy.

Recognizing the Difference

The difference between the two is where you are going to make your money. You don't want the open gap to be too large or too small because that will make it harder for you to figure out a path forward. Once you have found a suitable gap between the two assets, that is the difference that you will want to exploit. After you have done it once, it will be easier for you to repeat going forward. You can continue using the same template as you trade more options.

Act Accordingly

Finding assets that have gaps and recognizing that there are gaps that you can profit on are just the first parts of the co-integration strategy. You will need to recognize which asset is *causing* the gap – it is often due to the temporary weakness of a stock or a sudden surge for another, though there can be many reasons. As best as possible, identify what the reason is and then buy a call if you believe that a stock is oversold by the market, or buy a put if you think that a stock is experiencing a temporary surge and will soon fall.

Point of Exit and Profit

The point where the gap closes is the point of exit. This is the point that you will be looking for each time that you use this strategy. If you want to make sure that you are getting the most out of the co-integration strategy, all you need to do is cash in on the point of exit. If you are attentive and work strategically with your binary options, you can even begin predicting the timing of the point of exit.

CHAPTER 7:
Selecting a Trade Partner

What is it you that look for when you are considering opening a live (funded) trading account? First, a reliable platform, for me reliable means that when it's time to trade the platform is working, also meaning that you can get steaming (tradable) prices which allows you to buy and sell with ease. If you are trading with a broker that has a platform that is down more than a couple times a year, then you definitely want to consider switching, it really shouldn't be that they are down more than maybe once a year, because most platforms are up all the time.

Next thing you want to look at is what I call good liquidity over numbers. When I mention "numbers" I am referring to if you are looking to do news trading, for example, over job report numbers, interest rate reports, housing numbers. There are many traders where more or less a lot of their strategy is based on trading as we call it in the business, "over numbers." This is trading in the middle of market news reports and this is also the time when you can actually get into this type of liquidity squeeze. In a concrete example with needing good liquidity over numbers, let's say that the Bank of England rate decision is announced, you are attempting a trade, and when you try to buy or sell your broker keeps requoting the prices or maybe they won't even allow you to execute. If you are experiencing this on a regular basis, you should consider trading elsewhere because you should be able to get trading done even over news reports.

Finally, you definitely want to speak to your friends, if your friend is a heavy options trader, find out about his experiences with his broker. Because usually this a good source of how they (the broker) are when you need to trade. You will also want to know about the process when there is a need to transfer money to the account or from the account. What has been your friend's experience? has it been pretty smooth or has there been a lot of administration and they needed to send many emails in order to accomplish this.

In review of the things that you need in selecting a good trading partner, a reliable platform, good liquidity over market reports, and feedback from your friends.

BONUS:
Tech Analysis Trade Guide

As promised there is much more to this book than the content that you have read so far. This exclusive technical analysis guide provides expanded content on forex, stocks, and commodities binary options strategies. You will get the maximum benefit by combining the content you have read so far with the tech analysis guide.

Chart Time Frame

Time frame, the most critical factor of a trading decision. The decision to buy or sell <u>always</u> begins with the time frame. A signal to buy or sell for a day trader is different from a swing trader and in a most cases extremely different from a long-term trader/investor. The examples we will use are based on short term/day trading time frames.

Day trading – Closing positions within 24 hours

Swing trading – Holding trades open from a few hours to maximum a few days

For short-term traders a chart setting of 1 hour is good for getting a market overview, and then making the decision to trade off the 30 or 15 minutes chart. The shorter your trading time horizon the shorter you chart time frame.

To use the settings above it's recommended that you create charts of different time frames and leave them open on your trading platform. This will make it more efficient to trade.

Time frame & your location in the buy - sell channel

Once the time frame has been set, you need to locate out where you are in the trade channel (the trade channel is the area between the high and low bands of the Bollinger Bands). If you are near the top of the channel that indicates that you are close to a potential reversal level (where the market turns/reverses), ex. if heading up, it suddenly heads down. If at the bottom and the market heads up it's also a reversal level.

What to do at reversal levels

This is where trading gets a bit tricky. Just because we are at or near a reversal level it's no guarantee that it will reverse. We could also get a breakout (the market going above/below known resistance or support levels). One tip in figuring out what to do next, is to simply review the chart for past market movements (did it go up or down) at the price level you are looking to see what happened in the market the last time. This is important because the central "person" here is the market not you).

For example, if the market headed down then there is a good chance that it will do that again. However this is NOT a guarantee, and you also need to be aware of fundamental data (news report, economic data) as this could throw everything off from the result of the last time.

If you don't have a position open already, and the market is at a potential reversal level, one way to trade it is setting a buy order above the reversal level. Therefore, if the market does get the breakout then you are in. The buy order is also part of your risk management because there is only money on the table if it gets executed and becomes a trade.

After figuring out where you are in the buy/sell channel you now want to pay attention to the RSI and what it is telling you. You need to have a match between that and your trade execution. So if the RSI is at overbought levels and you are near reversal levels on the Bollinger bands then it is a sign of a good potential sell opportunity.

Ideal buy signals

Ideally on a buy signal you want your RSI to be heading up from at or near the 30-40 levels giving good room/opportunity to head up. At the same time you also want the market to be located/trading near the bottom of the channel in the Bollinger Bands.

Finally, if using candlestick charts you will want them to be green (prices closing up). As you can see we need to see the same data (up) from our tools. Looking at red candlesticks (prices closing lower) and overbought (excessive buying) RSI levels is a mixed signal. This tell you to "stand aside"... do not trade until things are clearer.

Ideal sell signals

An ideal sell signal is simply the opposite of the above. In other words, your RSI will be heading down from 70-80 levels. At the same time you also want the market to be located/trading near the top of the channel in the Bollinger Bands. Finally, if using candlestick charts you will want them to be red (prices closing down).

Wrapping up

Ideally you want to execute a trade from when things are as close to ideal as possible. When faced with grey areas/undecided I suggest that you use buy or sell orders. Orders are NOT trades so no money is at risk until they are executed. These orders will be placed near the ideal levels that you are seeking to trade from.

As I have stressed several times, ideal trade scenario or not, you always place a stop order. Unfortunately, even the world's best research is no guarantee of a profitable trade.

Settings for the technical analysis tools

RSI

One RSI, the default of 14 is fine for most FX, CFD, equity trading. However, with shorter term trading day trading or swing trading then 14 is not optimal. I suggest 7 for swing trading and down to 4 for day trading.

Bollinger Bands

The default settings seems to work best for most traders and I suggest that you keep this setting.

Moving Averages

We use 50, 100, 200. The 50 is the alert signal, 100 short term and 200 is the long term.

TRADING SIGNALS

BINARY TRADING SIGNALS SERVICES

Signals help traders by outsourcing the research process. Why would anybody need trading signals if binary trading is so simple? Predicting whether prices are going to rise or fall is tricky.

Trading signals are recommendations sent by email, SMS, etc. Traders are informed to place a trade with the expiration time and the strike price of the option. If you are confident of the accuracy of the signals service, you simply trade on the signals. You can also use the signals to reconfirm your own research.

ACCURACY IS NO GUARANTEE OF A PROFIT

Because signals from a providerare meant to be acted upon quickly. With fast markets, you only have a small window of opportunity. Most recommendations received will be valid up to an hour, some will only be good for a few minutes.

RELIABILITY OF TRADING SIGNALS

Signals are as good as the people behind them. They can either be a company of professional analysts or just veteran traders with years of experience. Check the reviews.

SIGNALS: Things to Consider

• THE PRICE

A higher price is not always an indication of how accurate a signals provider can be.

• UNBELIEVABLE CLAIMS

If you come across a provider who makes crazy claims about its services, stay away from them.

• BE AWARE OF FAKE RESULTS

Anything can be manipulated. Be cautious of screenshots posted by providers as proof of the accuracy of their services.

• REPUTATION AND TRACK RECORD

Always look for a provider with a good reputation and track record among your trading friends.

SUPPORT & RESISTANCE STRATEGY

SUPPORT & RESISTANCE STRATEGY

Markets are known to fluctuate, which makes it ideal for new traders to trade (Call/Put) binaries.

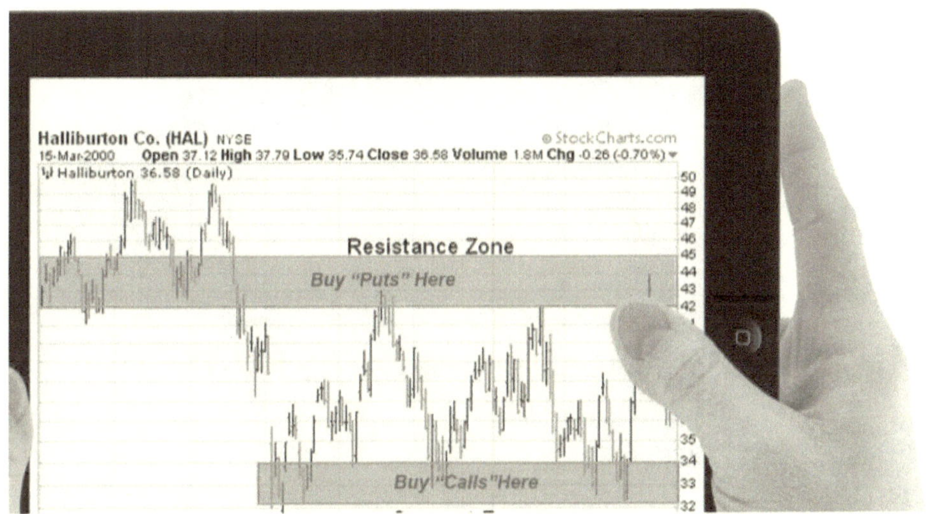

IMPLEMENTING THE STRATEGY

The beauty of the Support and resistance strategy is it is easy to understand and can be applied to any market. Buy a put at the resistance level or buy a call at the support level.

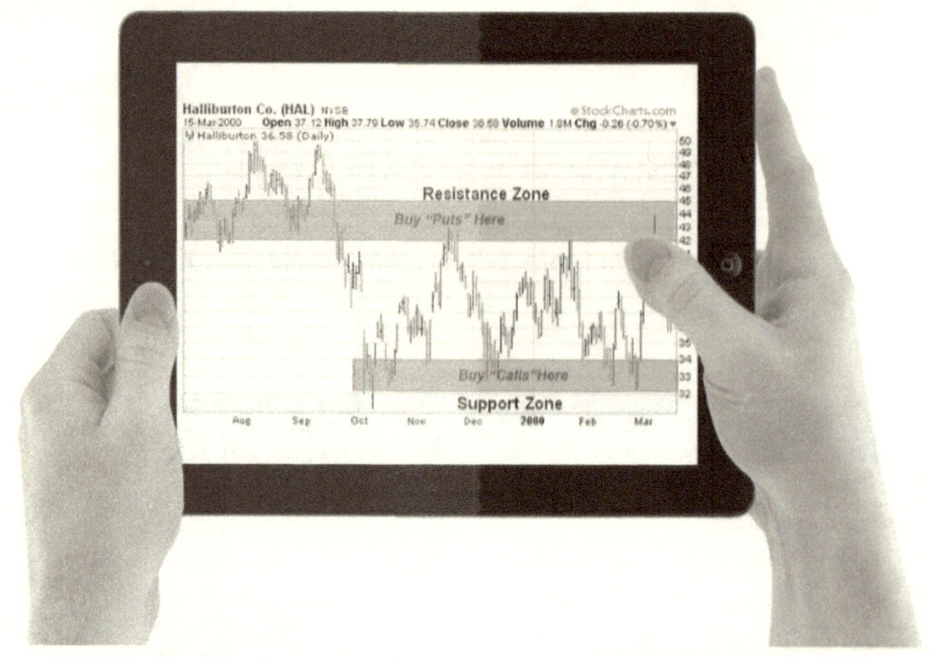

THE TRIANGLE BREAKOUT STRATEGY

TRIANGLE PATTERNS

Triangle patterns formed on price charts can be one of three types of shapes, symmetrical, ascending and descending.

SYMMETRICAL TRIANGLE

This chart pattern is formed as a result of indecision in the market. The tug of war between demand and supply ultimately causes the highs and lows of the asset's price to converge together and therefore forming this pattern.

To take advantage of such a neutral pattern? You purchase a call option above the slope of the lower highs and a put option below the slope of the higher lows. Regardless of which direction prices are heading, we will go with it.

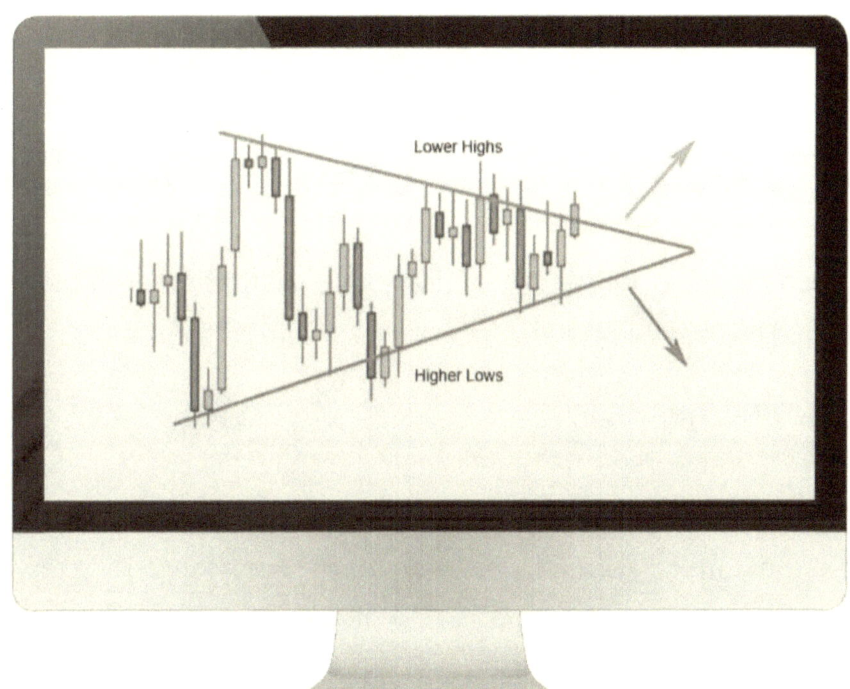

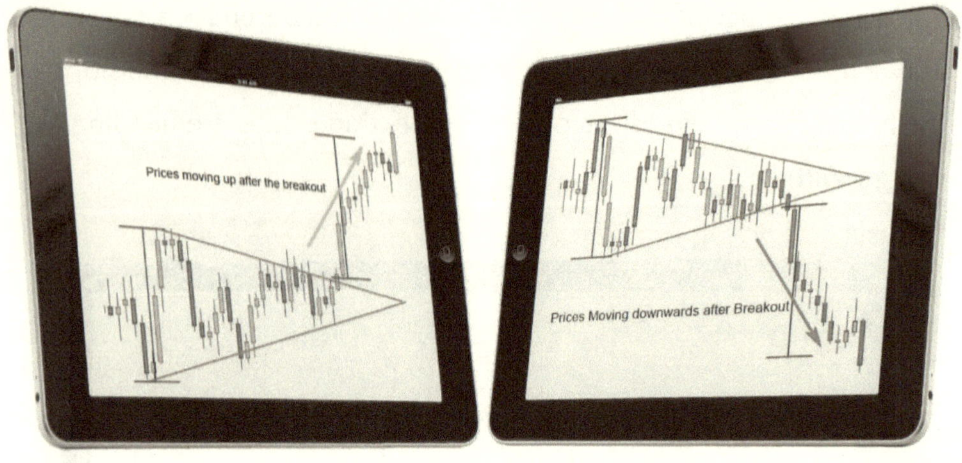

As soon as prices hit the first order, place another order in the same direction as the first hit order in order to maximize the breakout.

ASCENDING TRIANGLE

The pattern is a horizontal tread line at the top and an ascending trend line at the bottom. Formed when a series of higher lows rising towards a resistance line. The buyers in the market are gathering strength through the series of higher lows. Sooner or later a breakout will happen. Normally, prices will be on the uptrend since buying pressures are forcing the closing prices up, however it is possible that prices can go the other way.

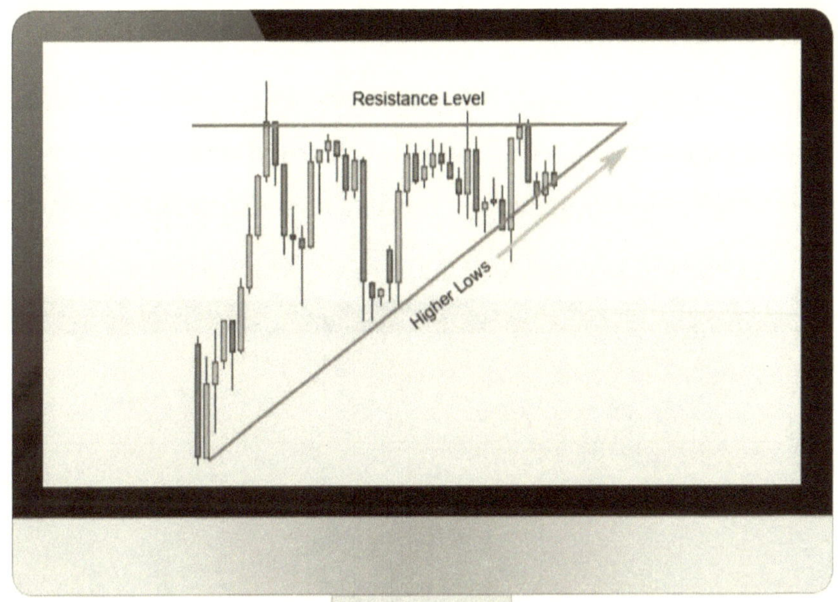

If we expect prices to be on the uptrend, buy a call option at or slightly above resistance level.

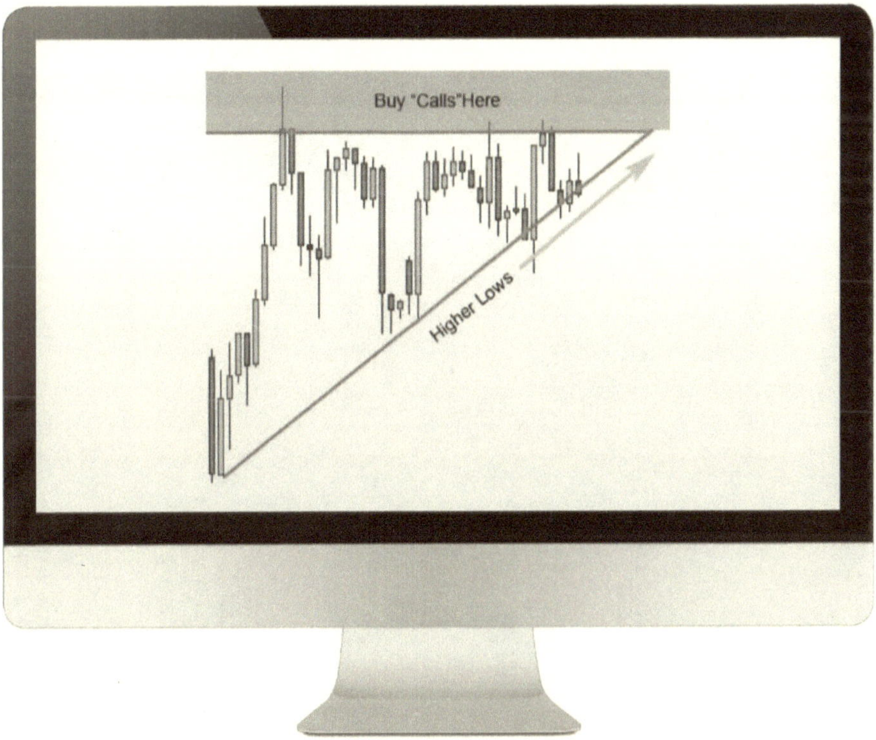

DESCENDING TRIANGLE

Characterized by downward sloping trend line converging towards a horizontal support level. This pattern is formed when selling pressure in the market is slowly gaining ground against demand (buying) forces.

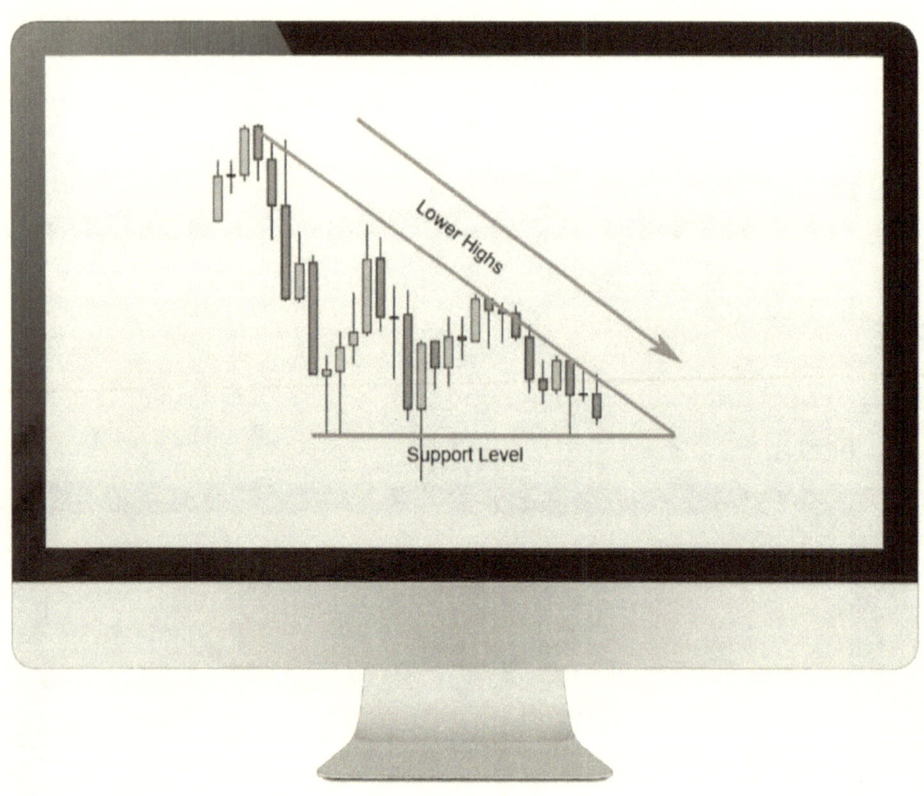

As selling pressure is forcing the opening prices down, it is highly likely that prices will break out in a downward trend. Since we are expecting that price will fall, purchase a put option at or slightly below support level.

CONCLUSION

Thank you for making it through to the end of *Binary Trading Strategies: Learn Binary Options Profit Making Strategies.* Let's hope it was informative and able to provide you with the first set of tools that you need to achieve your goals of trading with binary options and making money from them.

The next step is to test your skills at trading and build up your risk capital so that you can make additional trades. This will help you to have a better experience and give you the motivation that you need to succeed with binary options trading.

PROFILE OF THE AUTHOR

Wayne Walker is the director of a global capital markets education and consulting firm (gcmsonline.info). He has several years experience in leading and coaching teams of Investment Advisors and has managed top performing teams in the Private Client Group based on Bench Mark Earnings (BME).